What do you call an adolescent rabbit?

A pubic hare.

◆

What do you have when you have a hooker and two nuns on a football field?

One wide receiver and two tight ends.

◆

What's the difference between having a job for ten years and a wife for ten years?

After ten years, the job still sucks.

◆

How do you make a hormone?

Don't pay her.

◆

Why do WASPs throw their garbage away in clear plastic bags?

So that Puerto Ricans can go window-shopping.

◆

Why did Richard Nixon see the movie *Deep Throat* three times?

Because he wanted to get it down pat.

TURN THE PAGE FOR MORE *OUTRAGEOUSLY OFFENSIVE JOKES!*

Books by Maude Thickett

Outrageously Offensive Jokes I
Outrageously Offensive Jokes II
Outrageously Offensive Jokes III
Outrageously Offensive Jokes IV

Published by POCKET BOOKS

Outrageously OFFENSIVE JOKES II

MAUDE THICKETT

PUBLISHED BY POCKET BOOKS NEW YORK

Another *Original* publication of POCKET BOOKS

POCKET BOOKS, a division of Simon & Schuster, Inc.
1230 Avenue of the Americas, New York, N.Y. 10020

ISBN: 0-671-63435-6

First Pocket Books printing February 1984

10 9 8 7 6 5

Printed in the U.S.A.

For James Watt

Acknowledgments

I would like to thank everyone listed in my first book, since most everyone there contributed to my second. Here are a few new, outrageous people I'd like to name:

Renny N. and Pauline G., Mike O., Tom O., Sue and Joe S., Kate F., Carol D., Bonny P. Barbara H., Irving and Marilyn S., Jake and Pals, Johnathen the Temp, Marvin S., and just for a worthy effort Pierce. And special thanks to Jack Vallier and Lew Downard.

Contents

Celebrities

Have you heard about the Christmas cards James Watt plans to send to all his former government associates? The greeting reads:

Roses are reddish,
Violets are bluish;
If it weren't for Christmas,
We'd all be Jewish.
My sincere apologies,
James Watt

♦

Why did Richard Nixon go to see the movie *Deep Throat* three times?

Because he wanted to get it down pat.

♦

What vegetable will not be served this summer in Newport, R.I.?

Sunny Von Bülow.

♦

Why does Nancy Reagan always climb on top?

Because Ronnie can only fuck up.

♦

What do a male prostitute and the Pink Panther have in common?

They're both peter sellers.

♦

What do the Long Island Railroad and Jimmy Carter have in common?

They both pull out of Roslyn at approximately 5:30 A.M.

♦

A little boy who had a red wagon with several tiny puppies in it kept walking back and forth in front of the White House, and Reagan became very curious. The president went to talk to the little boy. "What kind of puppies are they?"

"Republican puppies," the little boy said.

Ronnie got quite a charge out of that and thought it real cute.

A couple of weeks later the little boy was again out walking in front of the White House with the puppies. Ron went to Nancy and said, "Nancy, go out there and ask that little boy with the red wagon what kind of puppies he has. I think you'll find his answer very cute."

Nancy went out to the gate and asked the little boy what kind of puppies they were. "Well, they're Democratic," answered the boy.

Surprised, Nancy said, "I thought they were Republican puppies."

"Well, they were until they opened their eyes."

◆

Little Herve Villechaize, formerly Tattoo of "Fantasy Island," needed a place where his small friends could stay when they came to visit him. After finding a very run-down building near his estate, Herve renovated it by lowering the ceilings and dividing the rooms to make one into two. And since he had gotten the place so cheaply, he decided not to charge board. Do you know what he called his place?

Stay free mini-pads!

◆

What's the difference between Joan Rivers and a whoopee cushion?

A whoopee cushion is a funny stunt.

♦

What do you get when you cross Billie Jean King with Bo Derek?

A DC-10.

♦

Superman is on his way to a large reunion of superheroes being held in Miami Beach. He arrives two hours late; his clothes are a mess and he has definitely been in a fight. As he approaches his table, his good friend Batman yells, "Hey, Man of Steel, what happened to you?"

"Well, this is gonna sound crazy, but I was zipping along the coastline, making great time, when suddenly I look down and there, lying on the beach, is Wonder Woman—naked!"

"Wow!" says Robin. "What did you do?"

"What do you think I did, kid? Her legs were spread, so I figured I was in like Flynn. I dove like an eagle!"

"Boy, I bet she was surprised," says the Hulk.

Superman smiles weakly and says, "Yeah, but not as much as the Invisible Man was."

♦

What's yellow and sleeps alone?

Yoko Ono.

♦

Did you know that Roman Polanski cruises in a school bus?

But seriously, we really shouldn't make fun of him. His new wife just died—crib death.

♦

What did Helen Keller say when she was handed a cheese grater?

"Most violent book I ever read."

♦

How did Helen Keller discover masturbation?

Trying to read her own lips.

♦

President Reagan, after playing a round of golf at a Washington, D.C., country club, was taking a shower in the locker room. Reagan looked over at the guy next to him and realized it was O. J. Simpson. As they started to talk, Ron couldn't help but notice the enormous size of O.J.'s member.

"O.J., you just got to tell me the secret of how you got such a big pecker," beseeched the president.

O.J. was a little embarrassed but told the president, "Well, I really haven't done all that much to get it that way, except ever since I was a little boy, every night before I went to bed, I'd walk over to the bedpost with it in my hand. Then I'd give it three good raps—'wham, wham, wham!'"

"That's really interesting, O.J.," said Ron. "I think I'll give it a try sometime."

That night Ron was about to get undressed for bed when he remembered what O.J. had told him. Nancy was already asleep, so he didn't feel too ashamed as he stepped before the bedpost, dong in hand. Determined to give it a try, the president smacked his prick against the post. "Wham, wham, wham!"

Half awake, Nancy whispered, "Is that you, O.J.?"

◆

While on vacation, President Reagan wants a girl for the night. He has three beautiful girls sent up to his room: a blonde, a brunette, and a redhead. To the blonde he says, "I am the president of the United States. How much to spend the night with you?" She replies, "Four hundred dollars." "Too much," he says. Then he says to the brunette, "I am the president of the United States. How much to spend the night with you?" "Two hundred dollars," she says. Just then the redhead comes in and says, "Mr. President, if you can raise my skirt as high as taxes, get your thing as hard as times are now, and screw me the way you are screwing the people of America, it won't cost you a damn thing."

♦

Do you know why they keep having to turn Karen Ann Quinlan?

Moss keeps growing on her north side.

♦

What did Yoko say when she heard John had been shot?

Oh no.

♦

Why can't the rock group The Go-Gos have sex?

Because their lips are sealed.

♦

Have you been listening to the news lately? They've found the black box: the new Miss America!

♦

Do you know what brand of contraceptive the label- and fashion-conscious man is wearing?

Brooke Shields.

♦

What's Billie Jean King's latest advertising sponsor?

Snap-on Tools of America.

Hey, Leroy!

How do blacks catch sickle-cell anemia?

By licking the backs of food stamps.

◆

Did you hear that Universal is going to do an all-black western?

It's going to be called *Ride, Motherfucker, Ride*.

◆

What is black foreplay?

"Scream and I'll kill you!"

◆

NASA was getting flack about not having sent a black man to the moon, so on the next space shuttle a black was put on board. The decision was so sudden that the black astronaut hadn't even been briefed on what to do. The only instructions given him were to strap in, wait till the shuttle reached twenty-five thousand feet, and remove his helmet. The shuttle was on automatic pilot, and NASA felt any fool could man her.

On the way up, the black astronaut started to think about how NASA was treating him. The Token Black, he thought to himself. But how could he prove it? He needed solid proof! If he could only prove it, he'd expose NASA as racists.

At twenty-five thousand feet the astronaut removed his helmet as instructed. Suddenly he heard a noise from another part of the ship. He was shocked when he came across another passenger—a chimp dressed in space gear! He, too, had removed his helmet at the designated time, but he also seemed to have something in his hand.

As the black drew closer he found it to be a list. The ape had a list of instructions, and he, THE TOKEN BLACK, had none! The black stood in shock as he read the last item on the list:

1200 hours—FEED THE NIGGER

♦

Did you hear that the NFL is going to use green footballs next year? Did you ever hear of a black dropping a watermelon?

♦

Three black women are discussing their men.

"I call my man Nine," says the first woman, "'cause he's nine inches long and does it nine times a night."

"I call my man Ten," says the second woman, "'cause he's ten inches long and does it ten times a night."

"I call my man Crème de Menthe," says the third woman.

"What?" asks the first woman. "Ain't that a liqueur?"

"Yeah," replies the third woman. "Yeah, yeah, oh yeah."

♦

A black man wakes up one morning and is horrified when he looks in the mirror. His face and part of his neck are starting to fade, turning almost white. He quickly goes to see his doctor.

"Don't worry," says his doctor. "It's really a minor thing with you black people. It happens all the time." The doctor mixes up an awful-smelling brown mixture and hands it to the black guy. "Here, drink this and you'll be fine in a jiffy."

The black guy drinks the stuff down in one swallow. The doctor looks at him and says, "Hmm, not enough. Take some more."

"Shit, man, do I have to? That stuff is horrible-tasting!"

"Do you want to get better? Now drink two more glasses."

After finishing the two glasses, the black man looks in the mirror. "Hey, Doc, I look fine. I'm back to my normal color. But what was that stuff? I swear it tasted just like shit!"

"Right you are. You were a half quart low."

♦

Do you know why flies have wings?

So they can beat the blacks to the watermelon.

♦

Do you know what they call a black riding a palomino?

Leroy Rogers.

♦

A reporter walked up to Stevie Wonder and asked him how it felt to have been born blind. Stevie replied, "It could've been worse. I could have been born black!"

♦

Can you identify the following?

FI FO FO   FI FO FO FO

It's the new telephone number at the Chicago mayor's office.

♦

A social studies teacher asks her students to identify some common farm tools. Holding up a rake, the teacher searches for a volunteer. Little Leroy is the only one waving his hand. Leroy never answers a question correctly. But unfortunately none of the other students are raising their hands, so the teacher has to call on little Leroy.

"Why, teacher, everyone knows that there is a rake," answers Leroy.

Shocked, the teacher says, "Why, Leroy, that's very good. And can someone else tell us what this tool is?" This time the teacher holds up a spade.

After a short silence from the rest of the class, little Leroy again answers the teacher's question correctly. Pleased but still stunned, the teacher holds up the last of her tools. This time even little Leroy is stumped.

"Why, Leroy, I'm surprised at you. Don't you know this tool is called a hoe?"

Wide-eyed, little Leroy replies, "Why, teacher, that ain't no hoe! My sister, everyone says she's a hoe, and she don't look anything like that!"

♦

What do people in New York call sneakers on a black boy?

Felony Footwear.

♦

What do you have when two blacks are in a shoebox?

A pair of black loafers.

♦

An airplane carrying the pope, the president of the United States, a black scholar, and a Boy Scout is flying over the Atlantic Ocean when suddenly it runs out of fuel. The pilot appears before the four passengers and explains the situation.

"The problem is that, other than the parachute I have for myself, we have only three others on board. I'll leave it up to yourselves to decide who will make the supreme sacrifice." Having said this, the pilot returns to the cockpit.

Staring at the three parachutes stacked against the luggage, the four begin to argue who is to be saved.

"I am the leader of the largest religion in

the world," says the pope. "I must be saved!" Grabbing a parachute, the pope leaps from the plane.

"Well, I'm the president of the most powerful country in the world, so I, too, must be saved!" With this, the president is gone from the plane.

This leaves only the Boy Scout and the black scholar. The black turns wildly to the Boy Scout and says, "I am the smartest black man in the world, and my people need someone like me to look up to. So I, too, must be saved!" Snatching blindly at the last remaining parachute, the black lunges from the plane.

Finally the pilot returns from the cockpit and sees the Boy Scout looking quite satisfied with himself. There is even a smile on his face as he looks down and out of the plane.

"I can see you're content with your decision," says the pilot. "But tell me, can you really smile in the face of certain death?"

The Boy Scout turns to the pilot, his smile widening, and says, "I'm not smiling at death. I'm smiling because the smartest black man in the world just jumped from the plane with my knapsack!"

♦

Why did the black guy push his girlfriend

away when she said she wanted to give him a blow job?

Because he was afraid that it would mess up his unemployment benefits.

♦

Did you hear that the Atlanta Braves are threatening to move?

There's a shortage of batboys.

♦

A country sheriff is driving along a back road one day and comes across what's obviously the site of a terrible accident. But the only person around is a white teenager who has just finished filling in a large hole.

"What on earth happened here?" asks the sheriff.

"Well, sir, this truckload of blacks was crossing the train tracks and I guess they didn't see the train coming. It made an awful mess."

"What's the hole for, boy?"

"Being the good citizen that I am, I figured I'd clean up the place a bit, so I gave those black boys a decent burial."

"You sure they were all dead?" asks the sheriff.

Patting down the last bit of earth, the boy grins and says, "Well, to tell you the truth, Sheriff, three of 'em kept saying that they weren't. But then you know how them black boys lie."

♦

A black man died and started walking to heaven. In front of him, the road split. One sign read Straight to Heaven; the other said To Purgatory. He strolled right up to the Pearly Gates.

"Just a minute!" said Saint Peter. "You have to have done something pretty special to go straight to heaven. What have you done?"

"I married a white woman on the courthouse steps in Mobile, Alabama," the black man proudly replied.

"That is pretty special," agreed Saint Peter. "When did you do that?"

"Oh, about three minutes ago."

♦

Do you know why blacks and Chinese don't intermarry?

Because they're afraid their kids would be called chiggers.

♦

Did you hear about the little black boy who had diarrhea?

He jumped into his mother's freezer because he thought he was melting.

♦

What do you call three blacks sitting in a garden?

Fertilizer.

♦

A car full of white southern boys was speeding through a small Georgia town when they passed a parked sheriff's car. A chase ensued, during which the white boys' car crashed into the back of a car full of blacks who were stopped for a red light. The sheriff arrived at the scene and got out of his car. He walked over to the white boys and said, "All right, boys, how fast were those coons going when they backed up into you?"

♦

A teacher stands before her first-grade class one day during a spelling lesson. "Can anyone here tell me how to spell the word *before* and use it in a sentence?"

A little redheaded girl is chosen and she says, "*Before*, b-e-e—"

"No, I'm sorry, that's incorrect," says the teacher.

A little blond boy is then called on and he gives it a try. "*Before*, b-e-f-o-u—"

"Sorry," interrupts the teacher, "that's also incorrect."

Finally, Tyrone is called on. He is the only black child in the class. "*Before*, b-e-f-o-r-e, *before*," says Tyrone, looking pleased with himself.

"Very good, Tyrone. Now please use the word *before* in a sentence."

After a few minutes of thought, Tyrone says confidently, "Two and two be four!"

♦

A young black couple, out on their first date, are sitting under a tree in a neighborhood park.

"Oh, David, you have such big biceps!" Rita says.

"Not really. They measure twenty inches on the tape," he says.

"Wow," replies Rita. "How about your chest?"

"I think the last time I measured it, it was fifty inches on the tape."

"Gee, that's big! But how about your, er, well, er, you know . . ."

Surprised, David says, "You mean my prick? Why, that's two inches."

"Two inches!" exclaims Rita. "You mean on the tape?"

"No, I mean two inches from the floor."

◆

What's black and red and has trouble getting through a revolving door?

A black man with a spear through his back.

◆

What do KKK members thank the good Lord for every night?

Sickle-cell anemia.

◆

Why do blacks keep chickens in their backyards?

To teach their kids how to walk.

◆

Rastus told Liza one day, he said, "Liza, I'm going to blacktop you, and when I'm through I'm gonna turn you over and I'm gonna asphalt ya."

◆

Do you know what to call a black person with an IQ of 50?

Gifted.

♦

What's the difference between a pothole and a black?

You'd swerve to avoid a pothole, wouldn't you?

♦

If Tarzan and Jane were black, what would Cheetah be?

The smartest of the three.

♦

One day a black priest and a white priest were killed in a car accident. A few moments later, they found themselves at the gates of heaven. After a short wait, the priests were greeted by Saint Peter, who took their names and looked over his list.

"I'm sorry," said Saint Peter, "but there appears to have been a mistake. Neither of you is due here for some time yet." He paused. "I really don't know what to do—you see, God's away for the day." He paused again. "I'll tell you what," said Saint Peter. "I'll return you to earth—as anything you want to be—until God returns to clear this up."

"Well, isn't that nice," replied Father Flanagan, the white priest. "I'd very much like to be an eagle flying around over the Rocky Mountains. I was there once on vacation and was very impressed by the mountains and the eagles."

"Fine," said Saint Peter, and Father Flanagan disappeared. "And what about you, Father Washington?"

"We can be anything we want, right? And it won't affect whether or not we get into heaven?"

"That's right," replied Saint Peter. "Only the acts you committed before you died will be considered on the Judgment Day."

"Great," said Father Washington. "I'd like to be a stud." And he, too, disappeared.

The next day, God returned. Saint Peter quickly filled him in on the two priests.

"I see," said God. "And where did the white priest choose to go?"

"Down there," said Saint Peter, pointing to the Rockies. "He's an eagle."

"And where is the black priest?"

Saint Peter pointed to a spot east of the Rockies. "Down there," he replied. "Father Washington is on a snow tire in Detroit."

◆

A Chinese man walks into a bar in a black

neighborhood and says to the black bartender, "How about a jigger, nigger?" The bartender is outraged and starts to lecture the Chinese about the evils of racism and how since he himself is a member of a minority he should know better. Finally, the black suggests that they change places and see how it feels.

The Chinese and the black change places. The black leaves the bar and then returns, walking up to the bar exactly as the Chinaman did.

"How about a drink, Chink?"

The Chinese says, "Sorry, we don't serve niggers."

[illegible] neighborhood and search the black bar [illegible]
[illegible] about [illegible] trigger?" The bar [illegible]
[illegible]
[illegible]
[illegible]
know [illegible]. Finally the black suggests that
they change places and see how it goes.
The Chinese and the black change places.
The black leaves the bar and [illegible]
[illegible] the bar [illegible] the Chinese
[illegible].
"How about [illegible]?"
They [illegible] quarter [illegible]
[illegible]."

Maladies

What do you get when you sit on a stereo?

Steroids.

♦

What do promiscuous angels get?

Harpies.

♦

A man ran into his doctor's office one day, all excited. The nurse asked him what was wrong.

"I have something wrong with my pecker," replied the man.

The nurse told the man he couldn't enter the office yelling things about his private parts, and requested that he go outside, enter the office again, and say he had something wrong with, say, his ear.

The patient went outside and returned. "I have something wrong with my ear."

"And what exactly is wrong with your ear?" asked the nurse.

"I can't piss out of it," came the man's reply.

♦

If shrimp come over on shrimp boats, where do crabs come from?

The captain's dinghy.

♦

A young girl is getting married, so she goes to her doctor to find out which contraceptive she should use. After a lengthy discussion with him she decides on the diaphragm.

After two weeks of marriage, she comes back to the doctor and says she thinks she must be dying or something.

"What seems to be the problem?" asks the doctor.

"Well, Doctor, I seem to have this awful discharge down there."

"Are you using your diaphragm like I told you?"

"Yes, every time I have intercourse," she answers demurely.

"And what kind of jelly are you using?"

"Grape."

♦

A young woman arrives in the United States fresh off a ship from France. Her first stop is a drugstore, where she asks the druggist for some "medication for bugs in the bush."

Getting her drift, the druggist gives her the strongest remedy he has for the crabs.

A couple of weeks go by, and the Frenchwoman and the druggist meet on the street outside the store. He asks, with a sly smile, whether the bugs in the bush have gone. She replies, "Ah, monsieur, the bugs, they are gone; the bush, it is gone; and so, monsieur, is Pierre's mustache!"

♦

What do you call a legless man water-skiing?

Skip.

♦

A man with a draining boil at the crack of his ass goes to a doctor to seek help. The doctor asks the man to drop his pants so he can see the problem. "That is the most disgusting thing I have ever seen," the doctor says. "You are dripping pus and blood over everything. Please leave at once!"

In anger, the man leaves. He goes to a second doctor, but he, too, refuses to treat him.

By now desperate, the man consults a third doctor, claiming he has an emergency. The doctor looks at the draining boil and says that he also is unable to help the man, but a guy called Felix Pussucker is the one to see. The doctor tells the man that Felix can be found down at the shipyards.

After questioning several dockworkers, the man finds Felix, who asks him to drop his pants so that he can see the problem.

"All right, bend over and spread your cheeks," says Felix as he proceeds to place his mouth on the man's boil and suck out the pus. Felix is enjoying it immensely as pus and blood run down his chin. In the midst of this, the man produces a huge fart, right in Felix's face. Felix suddenly removes his face from the man's ass, turns him around, and, in obvious annoyance, says, "You know, it's guys like you that really make this job disgusting!"

♦

The doctor in our town is so bad that he treated a guy for yellow jaundice for five years before he realized the man was Chinese.

♦

What do you call a person who is psychoceramic?

A crackpot.

♦

Why do lepers like potato chips?

Because they can use the back of one another's heads as dips.

♦

A man who is having gas problems explains to his doctor that every time he farts it sounds like *honda.*

The doctor does an examination and finds nothing wrong with the man. As a last resort he looks into the patient's mouth and finally spots the problem. "I'm sorry, you'll have to go to a dentist for your problem."

So the man goes to see his dentist. After a quick exam the dentist announces that the man has an abscess. "No problem, I'll have you fit and without your embarrassing problem in a jiffy," says the dentist.

Sure enough, the man's problem disappears and he no longer makes farts that sound like *honda.* The next week the man calls up the dentist and thanks him for all he's done for him. But before he hangs up he asks the dentist how he knew the problem was caused by an abscess.

The dentist replies, "It's easy. Everyone knows abscess makes the farts go *honda!*"

♦

A man walks into a doctor's office and says, "Doc, you gotta help me. I need a prescription for Sex-lax."

"You mean Ex-lax, don't you?" asks the doctor.

"No. I don't have any trouble going, I only have trouble coming!"

Goldstein, Goldman, and Goldberg

Moses is up on Mount Sinai and he suddenly becomes very upset. With his face upturned to the heavens he says in disbelief, "Now let me get this straight: We're the chosen people and You want us to cut off the tips of our *whats?*"

♦

Two middle-aged Jewish women meet at a bingo game and start to discuss their families.

"So, Ruth, how is your eldest son, Irving?" asks Beth.

"Oh, he couldn't be better, thank you. He and his wife have three children now. They have a big house on Long Island and a condo in Florida. He's a pretty well-known dentist now, you know."

"That's beautiful," replies Beth. "And how's your other son, Stuart, the mentally retarded boy?"

"Oh, he's an attorney."

♦

A Jewish prospector down on his luck goes into town looking for sex. All the girls in the area want fifty bucks and he has only twenty.

A madam at one house tells him that she

knows a black hooker who might be interested for twenty dollars. If that hooker won't take care of him, the madam says, he should come back and she'll take him on herself. A half hour goes by and the Jewish man is back.

Years go by and the old Jew never forgets the madam. One day he is in the same area where he had met the madam and so he goes to her house. When she answers the door, she recognizes him right away. They sit and talk for a little bit, and finally the madam says she has someone she'd like the old Jew to meet. She calls in a young man about twenty years old and says, "David, I'd like you to meet your father."

The boy looks at the prospector and says, "Do you mean to tell me I'm half Jewish?"

Insulted, the old Jew says, "You ungrateful son of a bitch, if I had had another thirty bucks you'd be half black, too!"

◆

A Jewish man goes to see a shrink. He introduces himself as Napoleon Bonaparte, even though his file card lists him as Irving Levine.

"So what seems to be the problem?" the doctor asks his patient.

"Doctor, everything is wonderful. My army is strong, my palace is magnificent, and my country is prospering. My only problem is Josephine, my wife."

"Oh," says the doctor. "And what's her problem?"

Throwing up his hands in despair, the little Jew says, "She still thinks she's Mrs. Levine!"

♦

Why do JAPs use tampons instead of sanitary napkins?

Because nothing goes in without a string attached.

♦

What is a JAP breakfast?

A Tab and a jelly roll.

♦

A JAP goes to her doctor to get some relief from the bruises she has on her knees.

"Those bruises are awful. How did you get them?" asks the doctor.

Embarrassed, the JAP answers, "Well, you see, Doctor, when we, er, make love, er, well . . ."

"Oh, I understand," says the doctor. "You'll just have to change positions until those bruises heal."

"Oh no, Doctor, I can't do that. My dog's breath is murder!"

♦

One day a man goes to his JAP wife and wants to know how much she loves him.

"Darling," he asks, "would you still love me if I became disfigured?"

"I'll always love you," she says as she files her nails.

"How about if I couldn't make love to you anymore?"

"I'll always love you, dear," she replies, still concentrating on her nails.

"Well, how about if I lost my hundred-thousand-dollar-a-year-job? Would you still love me then?"

The JAP puts down her nail file, looks at her husband's anxious face, and says, "Darling, I'll always love you, but most of all, I'll really miss you!"

♦

This joke should be told with a Jewish accent.

Two elderly Jewish men meet in Miami. They are old friends, but they haven't seen each other in over a year.

"So, Saul, how are you?"

"Not bad."

"What have you been doing with yourself?"

"I got myself a hobby."

"A hobby? What kind of a hobby?"

"I keep bees."

"You keep bees? Where do you keep bees?"

"In my house. Where do you think?"

"In your house?"

"In my cellar."

"In your cellar, Saul? But don't they sting you?"

"Naw, I keep them in a closet in my cellar."

"In a closet! Don't they attack you when you open the door?"

"Don't be silly. I keep them in a jar with a lid on it."

"With a lid on it? Saul, don't they die?"

Saul looks at his old friend and says with a shrug, "Fuck 'em, it's only a hobby."

"To the house. Where do you [illegible]
are your house?"
"[illegible]"
"In your [illegible]? [illegible] you don't [illegible]
[illegible]?"
"Well, I keep them in a closet in my cellar."
"In a closet? Don't they attack you when you
open the door?"
"Not if I'm quick. I keep them in a jar with a
lid on it."
"With a lid on it. Gee! Don't they die?"
Paul looked at [illegible] and [illegible] with a
strange [illegible] [illegible] a [illegible]."

Various Villainies

What do you call an adolescent rabbit?

A pubic hare.

♦

What do you have when you have a hooker and two nuns on a football field?

One wide receiver and two tight ends.

♦

What did Jim Fowler do when he and a rhino came across each other in the African bush?

He wiped it off.

♦

When an elderly couple came into the judge's chamber and asked for a divorce, the judge was totally appalled. "I can't believe that you're here in my court. You people are ninety-four years old and you've been married for sixty-three years. Why didn't you divorce years ago if you were unhappy? I simply don't understand it."

The wife looked at the husband and the

husband looked at the wife. Finally, the husband turned to the judge and said, "Well, Judge, we decided to wait until the kids were all dead."

♦

Did you hear about Air Florida's new slogan?

"If you miss us at the gate, catch us in the bay."

♦

Why does New York have so much herpes and California so many real estate agents?

New York had first choice.

♦

A priest wanted to raise money for the church. He was told that there was a fortune in horse racing, so he decided to purchase a horse and enter it in a race. However, at an auction, the going price for a horse was so steep that he decided to buy a donkey and race him. To his surprise, the donkey came in third. The next day the racing sheet carried the headline PRIEST'S ASS SHOWS. The priest was pleased with the donkey and entered it in another race. This time it won. The paper reported PRIEST'S ASS OUT IN FRONT. The bishop was so upset with this kind of publicity that he ordered the priest not to enter the donkey in any more races. The newspaper read BISHOP SCRATCHES PRIEST'S ASS. This was just too much for the bishop, so he ordered the priest to get rid of the donkey. The priest gave the donkey to a nun at a nearby convent, and the headline read NUN HAS BEST ASS IN TOWN. The bishop fainted. He informed the nun that she would have to dispose of the donkey. She sold it to a farmer for ten dollars, and the paper duly recorded NUN PEDDLES ASS FOR TEN BUCKS. They buried the bishop the next day.

◆

What's the last thing that passes through a cat's mind as he's hit by a truck going a hundred miles an hour?

His asshole.

◆

A little man walks into a bar and sits down and orders a beer. He's sitting there drinking his beer, minding his own business. Next to him sits a really huge, Bubba Smith–type guy. All of a sudden the great big guy turns to him and, just whack, knocks the little guy off the bar stool, across the floor, up against the wall.

The little fellow doesn't know what hit him. He picks himself up and walks over to the bar stool and sits back down. He turns to the guy and says, "What on earth was that for?"

The big guy says, "That was my karate, from Korea."

The little fellow thinks, Well, this guy's wacko. I'm going to finish my beer and get out of here.

But all of a sudden the big guy turns on him again and, bang, knocks the little fellow off the bar stool, across the floor, up against the wall.

The little fellow doesn't know what hit him. He picks himself up and figures, This guy is definitely wacko. I'm going to finish my beer and get out of here. "What was that for?" he asks. "That was my judo from Japan," replies the brute.

The little fellow thinks, Well, it's time to exit. So he leaves. About a half hour later the little fellow peeks his head in the bar and the big guy is still sitting there. So he tiptoes up behind him and just goes wham! The big fellow is down and out cold.

The bartender walks up to see what's going on, and the little fellow looks at the bartender and says, "When that son of a bitch comes to, you tell him that was a crowbar from K-Mart."

♦

What do you call a man with a green ball in each hand?

Someone in perfect control of the Jolly Green Giant.

♦

My grandmother used to tell an old story about a radio broadcast of several years ago during which the audience was asked questions and were given a box of Snicker bars for the answers. One evening during the live broadcast the master of ceremonies started talking to a newlywed couple. He leaned over and asked the woman, "What's the first thing you said on your honeymoon?" The wife thought for a minute and said, "Oh, I can't, that's hard." And the man said, "Give this lady a box of Snickers!"

♦

A little boy walked into an ice-cream store wearing a cowboy hat and a pair of six-shooters. He asked the clerk for an ice-cream sundae. The clerk asked, "Do you want your nuts crushed?"

The little boy whipped out his guns, pointed them at her, and said, "Do you want your tits shot off?"

♦

What do you get when you cross a whore and a computer?

A fucking know-it-all.

♦

A visibly shaken man staggers into a bar. He asks the bartender for a double Jack Daniel's. After downing the first drink, he proceeds to down two more doubles.

The bartender becomes concerned and asks the man what his problem is. The man mumbles that it's not important, that no one can help him anyway. The man then orders his fourth drink, and again the bartender asks if there is anything he can do.

This time the man says, "Yeah, there is something you can do. Answer me a question. How big is a penguin?"

The bartender holds his hand about three feet off the ground and says, "About this high. Why?"

"Shit, I think I just ran over a nun, that's why."

♦

A traveling salesman's car breaks down, so he goes for help to a nearby farmhouse. He sees a little boy in the front yard and asks where his mother is. The boy shakes his head in a beckoning motion and leads the salesman toward the backyard.

The salesman gets there only to find the mother making out with a goat. Revolted, he turns to the boy and says, "Do you know what your mother is doing?"

The little boy just nods.

"Well, doesn't it bother you?"

"NAA NAA NAA NAA. . . ."

◆

Jesus is in a town where the townsfolk are about to stone a woman for committing adultery. "Let him without sin cast the first stone," he proclaims to the crowd.

From the crowd steps an old woman who flings a huge boulder at the adulteress, killing her instantly.

Jesus looks at the old woman and shakes his head in disgust. "You know, Ma, you really know how to piss me off."

◆

The town drunk was always mooching drinks at the local saloon. The bartender, getting tired of his begging, told him that he would give him a free drink if he would take a sip out of the spittoon. The drunk, wanting a drink badly, picked up the spittoon and gulped and gulped and gulped. Setting up a drink, the bartender remarked that he had only wanted him to take a sip. Downing his drink, the drunk replied, "I know, but it was in one long string."

♦

FAA officials were thrilled when they found the black box that had been in the Air Florida plane that crashed in January of 1982. What follows is a transcript of the part of the tape that was not released to the media.

Copilot: Sir, we don't have enough thrust. We don't have enough altitude. And it looks as if we've got ice on our wings.

Pilot: Don't worry about it. We'll cross that bridge when we get to it.

♦

What's black, pink, and hairy and sits on a wall?

Humpty Cunt.

♦

How come there isn't any grass in the stadiums in Iowa?

So the cheerleaders don't graze during halftime.

♦

Where do female copilots sit in an aircraft?

In the cuntpit.

♦

What do you call a female peacock?

A peacunt.

♦

A young man who could never hold on to his money goes off to college one day. But only a month later his money is gone, and he has to ask his father for more. His father agrees to send some but warns him to be careful since no more will be sent. Sure enough, though, the boy spends everything and tries to think of a scheme to get more from his pop. Remembering that his father would do just about anything for the family dog, the boy calls his father and says, "Dad, there's a professor here who will teach Baron to speak for a thousand bucks." After some persuasion the father agrees to send Baron for speech lessons.

A couple of months go by, and again the young man runs out of money, so he calls his father again. But this time he says, "Dad, Baron did real well with the speech lessons, so the professor feels Baron is ready for the next step. For another thousand bucks he'll teach Baron to read." Again his father is persuaded, and the money arrives.

The year finally ends, and the boy makes plans to go home, but of course Baron cannot speak or read. Desperate, the boy gives Baron away to a nice family and then makes a phone call to his dad.

"Dad, I've got some bad news for you, but it's a little bit of a story, so sit down.

"I was in the john shaving, and Baron was next to me reading the *Times* when suddenly he says, 'Gee, do you think your mother will ever find out about all the times Dad fucked around with his secretary?'

"Dad, I got so nervous that my hand slipped, and the razor flew out of my hand. I don't know how it happened, but the razor slit Baron's throat and he's dead."

After a brief silence his father asks, "Are you sure?"

◆

Mrs. McDonald was known for her Boston bean soup. When her secret for success was asked for, she replied that she used only 239 beans.

"How come only 239?"

"Because one more would make it too farty."

♦

The emperor was trying to find the best samurai swordsman in the land, so he had a contest. Only three samurai were confident enough to compete. The emperor looked over the three strong men and said, "I have here, in each of three containers, a fly. As I let the flies out one at a time, each samurai is to kill one as quickly as possible." All three nodded their understanding and assent.

The first samurai stood up, and the emperor opened the lid of the container. Out buzzed a fly, and whoosh!, quicker than you could imagine, the fly fell to the ground, deftly split in two. The crowd that had gathered in the court applauded.

The second samurai stood, and the emperor opened the lid of the second container. Out buzzed another fly. Even quicker than the first samurai, the second whirled his sword whoosh! whoosh!, and the fly fell to the earth in four pieces. The crowd cheered.

As the third samurai rose to the challenge, everyone wondered what he could do to top the feats of the last two swordsmen. When the emperor opened the lid of the third container, the samurai, poised for action, made a graceful wave of the sword, and the fly buzzed off.

The emperor, furious to think he was being mocked, cried, "What do you think you're doing? That fly got away!"

"I know," replied the samurai, "but he'll never fuck again!"

♦

Why is shit tapered at both ends?

So your asshole doesn't slam shut when you're going.

♦

What do you get when you cross a whore and a Smurf?

A fucking little kid three feet high.

♦

Do you know how a Beverly Hills housewife calls her kids to dinner?

"Get in the car."

♦

Do you know what a Beverly Hills housewife wears to a funeral?

A black tennis dress.

♦

A woman comes running into the town sheriff's office screaming in fright.

"Sheriff, the ape from the circus escaped, and it's on my roof!"

"I know just the guy to call," the sheriff says. "We'll be right over."

In less than ten minutes the sheriff and another fellow arrive. The man is carrying a pair of handcuffs and a shotgun, and is leading a very mean looking dog. As they arrive, they spot their quarry. The sheriff turns to the man and says, "Okay, what's the plan?"

"Well," says the guy, "I'll go up on the roof, make some kind of disturbance, and try to scare him off the roof. When the ape falls off the roof, the dog is trained to run right up to him and bite his nuts off. The ape will be in such terrible pain that you can just walk up to him and handcuff him. That's all there is to it."

The sheriff then says, "Well, that sounds pretty easy, but what's the shotgun for?"

"That's in case I fall off the roof first, you're going to shoot that fucking dog!"

♦

Why do babies have soft spots on their heads?

So in case there's a fire at the hospital, the nurses can carry them out five to a hand.

♦

It was my father's birthday and I wanted to buy him a bird dog, so I went to the pet store. The owner of the pet store had a bird dog, but it cost a thousand dollars. I couldn't believe a bird dog cost a thousand dollars. The owner of the pet store said it was a special dog: this dog could tell you just how many birds are in the bush. "I'll prove it to you," he said. So he went and got the dog and we went out back. The owner let the dog loose and the dog went up to a bush and started shaking his head. The dog shook his head five times. The owner said, "There are five birds in the bush." He went up to the bush and shook it, and out flew five birds. I said, "I still don't believe it." So the owner said, "We'll show you again." So again he let the dog loose and the dog went up to a bush and shook his head three times. The owner went up to the bush and shook it, and three birds flew out. Well, I was almost ready to believe him, but I thought that it really must be a trick. So the owner took me farther into the woods and set the dog loose again. The dog started running around a bush wildly, humping, and shaking the shit out of a wooden stick he had found nearby. I didn't know what the hell was going on. So I said to the owner, "What the hell is this dog doing running around the bush and humping and shaking the shit out of that stick?" The owner said, "Don't you know what he's trying to tell you?" "No," I said. The owner said, "He's trying to tell you that there are more fucking birds in that bush than you can shake a stick at."

♦

A preacher was walking down the street when he came across a little black boy and his little puppy. The preacher stopped him and said, "What a cute little puppy dog you got there." The little boy said, "Thank you, Preacher." The preacher said, "Do you mind if I ask you what you call your little puppy dog?" The little boy said, "I call him Porky." The preacher asked, "Why do you call your little puppy dog Porky?" Looking down at his dog, the little boy replied, "Because he likes to fuck pigs."

♦

A well-endowed woman entered a chic Fifth Avenue store. After trying on hundreds of very expensive evening gowns, she asked the exhausted clerk if she could try on a very sexy, low-cut gown that was being displayed in the store window. Since the gown in the window was the only one left in the store, the poor salesclerk had to go through a lot of trouble to undress the window dummy. Clenching her teeth, the salesclerk handed the woman the gown and watched her try it on. Finally the woman turned to the salesclerk and said, "Well, how do I look? Do you think it's cut low enough to show off my marvelous breasts?" The clerk took one look and said, "It looks great, but do hairy chests run in your family?"

♦

What's brown and sounds like a bell?

Dung.

♦

What do you call a female sex-change operation?

Addadicktomy.

♦

The boss of a large lumberyard is approached by an elderly blind man who is inquiring about a job. "Sorry, fella, you'd have to be able to tell the difference between all the different types of wood we carry, and frankly speaking, you not being able to see and all . . ."

"No problem, young man; I can determine different woods by just smelling their scent," the blind man says confidently.

Unable to believe this, the boss man has two of his assistants bring out a two-by-four pine and hold it directly under the old blind man's nose. Without touching the wood, the old man takes a hearty sniff and declares the wood to be pine.

Amazed, the boss has another piece of wood brought out. This time it is oak. After sniffing at the wood under his nose, the blind man states it is most definitely oak.

"One more test, old man," says the boss. But instead of wood, his naked secretary is brought out. She, too, is held under the old blind man's nose. She is held aloft by both hands and feet with her pubic hairs almost tickling his nose.

"Can you flip this one around for me once? This one is tough."

After a few more sniffs and a few more moments of thinking, the old blind man makes his decision.

"Well," says the old man, his face breaking into a grin, "you tried to put one over on an old blind man, but it didn't work. You can't fool this nose, no siree! This here piece of wood is without a doubt the shithouse door off a tuna boat!"

Eye-talians, or Never Let a Dago By

What is an Italian virgin?

A girl who can run faster than her brother.

♦

What do Pete Rose and a Mafia don have in common?

Three thousand hits.

♦

What do you get when you cross an Italian with an Aggie?

A hit man who misses.

♦

At a social gathering, Mrs. Goldberg corners Mrs. Tanelli near the refreshment table. Mrs. Tanelli has just moved to America from Italy. After listening politely for what seems like ages, Mrs. Tanelli starts to get a little impatient.

"And on our tenth anniversary my darling husband gave me a beautiful full-length mink," boasts Mrs. Goldberg.

"That'sa nice," Mrs. Tanelli replies.

"On my twentieth anniversary my husband gave me a three-karat cocktail ring," Mrs. Goldberg continues.

"That'sa nice," Mrs. Tanelli answers again.

"And what wonderful things has your husband done for you?" Mrs. Goldberg asks.

"Well, right after we come to America, my husband he send me to a very expensive finishing school."

"Really? And what did they teach you at the school?" pries Mrs. Goldberg.

Looking Mrs. Goldberg straight in the eye, Mrs. Tanelli says, "Well, I usedta say bullshit. Now I say that'sa nice."

♦

What's this?

U, 2 wedding   Maria Mr.

(You comma to wedding—Maria missed her period.)

♦

Define *psychopath.*

An Italian millionaire in a bordello.

♦

Dracula goes to Rome and checks into the Grand Italia Hotel. The bellhop, after bringing in his coffin, asks if there is anything else he can do for him. Dracula says, "Yes, there is," and lunges for the boy's throat. After draining the blood from him, Dracula throws the bellhop's lifeless body out his bedroom window. The body lands on a policeman stationed in front of the hotel. The impact sends the policeman sprawling to the ground.

Meanwhile Dracula still has not satisfied his bloodlust, so he goes into the hotel's hallway and grabs a chambermaid. When finished with her, he throws her drained body out the same window. This body, too, lands on the unfortunate policeman, who has just managed to dust himself off after the first assault. This time, though, he is knocked cold.

A half hour later the police commissioner arrives on the scene and manages to get the unconscious officer back to his senses. "Officer Vetillo, can you explain what is going on here?" the commissioner asks as he looks at the dead drained bodies on the ground.

"I don't honestly know, sir. All I know is that drained wops keep falling on my head."

♦

An Italian couple are driving along a road one night when they run out of gas. As they pull off the road, the boy says to the girl that he might as well take a leak while they're stopped.

As he gets out, the girl thinks to herself that this must be some kind of scheme to get her alone in the backseat. She decides to check out whether they really have run out of gas, so she goes around to the gas-tank nozzle. Opening it, she tries to smell for fumes. Smelling none, she strikes a match. BAM! The tank explodes and the couple are blown into the bushes.

Coming to, the girl says, "Help me find my purse. It has my money in it."

The boy moans, "Aw, fuck your purse. Help me find my hand—it has my prick in it!"

♦

How many Italian mechanics does it take to give your car a lube job?

Only one if you hit him right.

♦

An American Indian goes to his doctor and tells him that he is tired of being held back because of his race. The Indian says he has heard of a certain clinic where one's physical features can be altered so radically, that one can officially be considered to belong to another nationality.

His doctor says yes, he has heard of such a place, but the procedure is very expensive. How much can he afford? The Indian says two hundred dollars is all he has. After checking with the clinic, the doctor learns that for two hundred dollars, Polish is the best nationality they can give him. Almost any other race would be much more expensive. The Indian says he doesn't care, and his appointment is made.

Before the operation is performed, the surgeon comes to see his patient. "Running Deer, I want you to know how serious this operation is. Since the average Pole has less brainpower than most people, we will have to remove forty percent of your brain. So I want you to be sure that this is what you want." Running Deer doesn't hesitate at all and tells the doctor to go through with the operation.

After the operation, the first person Running Deer sees is his surgeon, looking very glum.

"Running Deer, I have some bad news. I was letting a young intern work on you, and his hand slipped. By complete accident the intern removed seventy-five percent of your brain."

Shocked, Running Deer says, "Mama Mia!"

♦

When the mate of a female gorilla in the Chicago zoo dies suddenly, a replacement is desperately needed. After all attempts to get another male gorilla fail, the zookeeper is frantic. The female's heat is almost over, and it will be months before she can be mated again. Traveling home one day, the zookeeper sees an Italian construction worker without his shirt on. The man is covered with hair. "Why not?" thinks the zookeeper, and he approaches the construction worker.

"How would you like to make an easy five hundred bucks?" asks the zookeeper.

"Who do you want killed?" asks the Italian warily.

"No one. You just got to make it with a gorilla at the zoo. No one would even have to know."

"What, are you fuckin' crazy? Get the hell out of here!" yells the Italian.

"Well, if you change your mind, here's my card."

When the Italian gets home he is still angry and he tells his wife what happened.

"Stupid! You know what I could do with an extra five hundred bucks! Call that nice gentleman up and tell him you'll do the job."

So, reluctantly, he calls the zookeeper. "Okay, I'll do it," says the Italian. "But I want you to know there are three conditions."

The zookeeper is ecstatic and says, "Anything, you name it."

"One, I'm only doing it once."

"Fine," says the zookeeper.

"Two, I'm not gonna kiss her."

"No problem."

"And three, if there are any children, they must be brought up Catholic."

♦

Did you hear about the new Italian tanks?

They have one speed forward and four in reverse.

♦

A Mafia don, after checking his books, realizes there is a thief among his family. The don calls in his most trusted aide, his first lieutenant, Dominick. "Dominick, find out who the thief is and bring him to me."

The next day Dominick informs the don that the thief has been uncovered. "I am saddened to tell you, Don, that the thief is Nunzio, the deaf-mute."

Astonished but furious, the don has the lieutenant bring the old deaf-mute before him. But since Nunzio can only communicate by means of sign language, Dominick must act as translator.

"Ask him where he has put the money, Dominick."

Using sign language, Dominick translates to the wide-eyed and frightened old man. The old man answers that he knows nothing about any money. Nodding, Dominick tells the don this.

Angered, the don takes a gun from his desk

and places it to Nunzio's now-sweating brow. In a threatening voice he orders Dominick to tell the deaf-mute that unless he comes clean he's going to blow his brains out.

After Dominick finishes translating, Nunzio panics. Realizing the don is a ruthless killer, Nunzio confesses to Dominick. With fingers flying Nunzio says, "Please, don't kill me! The money is in a green garbage bag in my cellar. A thousand pardons, don!"

When Dominick doesn't translate immediately, the don questions his lieutenant for an answer. Without the slightest hesitation Dominick turns to the don and says, "He says you don't have the balls to shoot him."

♦

The first day of school the new teacher says to her class, "All right, children, I want you to know that I have a very difficult name and I'm going to spell it out for you on the blackboard. Tomorrow, if any of you can remember how to spell it right, you'll get a bag of candy." The teacher turns to the board and writes, MY NAME IS MISS PRUSSY.

Little Enzo, who is just over from Italy, really wants to do well in his new school, so that night he goes home repeating over and over, "Prussy, Miss Prussy."

Enzo's older brother hears him and asks him what he's doing. Enzo explains, and his brother says with a grin, "That's easy to remember. Just think of pussy with an *r*."

The next day in class, Enzo is anxiously waiting to be called on. He has practiced all night and is ready to impress his teacher and his friends. The teacher looks out into the class and spots Enzo's waving hand. "Okay, Enzo, do you remember what my name is?"

In a sudden panic, Enzo tries to think of what his brother told him and stutters, "It's uh, uh, um, uh, CRUNT!"

♦

Why did the Italian staple his nuts together?

Since he couldn't lick 'em, he felt he should join 'em.

♦

Two Italians, Tony and Joe, meet on the street one night.

"Hey, Joe, where you going?"

"I'ma going to night school. You think I wanna be stupido like you?"

Angered, Tony says, "Oh yeah? Well, what do you learn in school?"

"Do you know who Georga Washing Machine is?"

"No, who?" asks Tony.

"He was the first presidente. Do you know who Abraham Linguine is?"

Embarrassed, Tony again answers, "No, who?"

"Boy, you are stupido," says Joe. "He was the presidente who freed all the eggplants."

Now Tony gets so angry about being called stupid that he says to Joe, "Hey, if you think you're so smarta, who is Luigi Gondrevorta?"

Joe thinks for a moment and says, "We haven't gotten to him yet. Who is he?"

Tony laughs and says, "See, you stupido, too. He's the one who's making love to your wife when you are at night school!"

♦

How do you brainwash an Italian?

Give him an enema.

In a Word, Sex

What did one congressman say to the other?

What page are you on?

♦

What's worse than a lobster on your piano?

Crabs on your organ.

♦

Did you hear about the nympho at the hotel pool?

She was barred from the area after the lifeguard saw her go down for the third time.

♦

When is it extremely dangerous to have a wet dream?

When you're under an electric blanket.

♦

A man comes home from work to find his wife standing at the top of the staircase. There she throws her leg over the banister and slides down.

"Hello, dear," she says as she climbs the stairs. Once at the top, she again slides down the banister.

Flabbergasted, he asks his wife, "What are you doing, darling?"

"Oh, nothing, really," she replies. "Just heating up dinner."

♦

A proud father gave his son twenty bucks and sent him off to the local whorehouse. On his way the boy passed by his grandmother's house, and she called him in. He explained where he was going, and she insisted that he save the twenty dollars and make love to her.

The boy returned home with a big smile. "How was it?" asked the father.

"Great, and I saved the twenty bucks," responded the boy.

"How's that?" his father asked.

"I did it with Grandma," the boy explained.

His father screamed, "You mean you fucked my mother?"

"Hey, why not? You've been fucking mine!"

♦

What's the difference between having a job and being married for ten years?

A job still sucks after ten years.

♦

A man works for many years in a pickle factory. He works the machine right next to the pickle slicer. At night he has kinky dreams about the pickle slicer. One day he goes bonkers and when he thinks no one is looking he starts to kiss the pickle slicer. Lust overpowers his senses and he puts his pecker in the pickle slicer. At that moment the boss happens to be passing by and sees the man attacking the pickle slicer. The boss calls the man a degenerate and fires him on the spot.

The man goes home and his wife asks him what he's doing home so early. He replies, "I went crazy and tried to make love to the pickle slicer. The boss saw me and fired me."

"Oh my God!" screams the wife, and pulls down her husband's pants to inspect the damage. Seeing none, she says, "Well, thank the Lord you weren't hurt. But what happened to the pickle slicer?"

The man smiles sheepishly and says, "The boss fired her, too."

♦

An astronaut lands on Mars and comes across a beautiful Martian woman stirring a huge pot over a flaming fire.

"What are you doing," he asks her.

"Making babies," she answers.

"That's not the way we do it on earth," he tells her.

"Well, how is it done there?" she asks him.

"I can't really explain it, but it's easy to show you. May I?"

She says yes, and he proceeds to show her how it's done. When they are finished she asks, "So where are the babies?"

"Oh, they don't come for another nine months," he tells her.

"So why did you stop stirring, then?"

♦

What's the hardest thing about performing a sex change from a man to a woman?

Inserting the anchovies.

♦

What do you do when your Kotex catches fire?

Throw it on the floor and tampon it.

♦

Former Presidents Jimmy Carter, Richard Nixon, and Jack Kennedy are on a boat sailing around the Cape, when all of a sudden the boat springs a leak and water starts pouring in.

Jimmy Carter cries, "Women and children first, women and children first!"

Nixon scowls. "Fuck the women and children."

Jack Kennedy: "Is there time?"

♦

What do you call the woman who makes the beds in a no-tell motel?

A Minute Maid.

♦

Mickey Mouse stood before the judge waiting for the verdict.

"Mickey Mouse, I cannot grant you a divorce, since the court has found Minnie Mouse to be mentally competent," proclaimed the judge.

"But, Your Honor, I didn't say Minnie was crazy. I said she was fucking Goofy!"

♦

Two friends were talking at a local bar one night.

"Man, was I lucky last night," said the first guy.

"What happened? Did you win the lottery or something?" asked the second.

"Naw, but last night I was banging my old lady, ya know, and right in the middle of everything, *wham!*, the goddam chandelier comes flying down on my ass!"

"You call that lucky?" asks his friend.

"Shit, yeah. If it had happened a couple of

minutes sooner I'd have broke my fuckin' neck!"

♦

A plane is flying over the Atlantic Ocean as the pilot is finishing an announcement on the intercom. Putting the mike down, he hits the Off switch. Unbeknownst to him, the switch is malfunctioning and his conversation is broadcast into the passenger area.

"Take over for a while, Dave," the pilot says to his copilot. "I think I'll go take a shit and then bang that new stewardess."

At this statement the passengers fly into a frenzy of conversation and gossip. The stewardess is greatly embarrassed and can no longer stay at her post, so she hurries toward the cockpit. But in her haste she trips and falls to her knees in the aisle. She happens to land next to a sweet little old lady, who turns to help her up. As she does, the lady says sweetly, "Don't rush, dearie; he said he had to take a shit first."

♦

Ginny and Joe are having a drink in Joe's apartment—their second date—and Joe is pouring Ginny a glass of wine.

"Tell me when," he says.

"After dinner," she replies.

♦

Do you know how married couples do it doggie style?

Without all the licking and sniffing.

♦

A little girl was sitting in a barber chair waiting for her first haircut. She was so frightened that she started to cry. The barber, experienced with children, gave the child a cookie. Her sobbing stopped, and so the barber began to cut her locks. But suddenly she started to cry again.

"What's the matter, little girl?" asked the barber. "Have you got hair on your cookie?"

"What are you—an asshole?" cried the little girl. "I'm only six years old!"

♦

A woman who was unhappy with the size of her breasts made an appointment with Dr. Schwartz, a breast specialist. After examining her, the doctor gave her a special cream to apply to her breasts.

"Now, listen carefully," Dr. Schwartz said. "These directions are very specific, and you must apply the cream always the same way. They may sound strange, but believe me, if you do it right, in no time you will be beautiful. Now, take your right hand, put a little cream in your palm, and apply it to your left breast, rubbing in a circular motion. As you are doing this I want you to chant, 'Mary had a little lamb.' Then add more cream to the same hand and move to your right breast, and keep rubbing in that same circular motion. On this breast you must chant, 'Its fleece was white as snow.' Keep rubbing and chanting until all the cream is absorbed. Do this entire procedure exactly as I have shown you four times a day for a month. When the month is up, you will have wonderful breasts."

So the woman goes home and every four hours she stops whatever she is doing and goes through the procedure. But one day she is in a shopping area when it is time to apply her cream. She runs to the parking area, hops into her car, and undoes her blouse. Applying her cream, she sings, "Mary had a little lamb, its fleece was white as snow."

Suddenly she sees a man in another car staring at her. Smiling, he shouts to her, "Do you go to Dr. Schwartz?"

Embarrassed, the woman nods her head yes.

"I thought so. So do I," the man replies.

And as the man turns away busying himself with something in his lap, the woman hears him sing, "Hickory, dickory, dock, the mouse ran up the clock."

♦

How do you make a hormone?

Don't pay her.

◆

What's white and found in women's panties?

Clitty Litter.

◆

You know you're getting old when your wife gives up sex for Lent and you don't find out until after Easter.

◆

How do you get a nun pregnant?

Fuck her.

◆

Two friends were walking on the beach one day when they saw a peculiar-looking man coming the other way. The stranger had an extraordinarily small head in comparison to the rest of his body.

"Excuse me, sir, I don't mean to be rude, but—" began the first friend.

"I know what you're going to ask me, and I don't mind telling you about it, because it was my own stupid fault," replied the stranger.

"One summer day, very much like today, I was walking along this very beach. In the sand I saw a very old looking bottle with a cork in it. Being terribly curious, I unplugged it. Sure enough, out comes this beautiful naked genie. She was the sexiest, hottest-looking dame I ever saw. So when she said she'd grant me any one wish I desired, I said 'How about a little head?' "

♦

Confucius say: Woman who fly airplane upside down has crack up.

♦

Definition of henpecked—a sterile husband afraid to tell his pregnant wife.

♦

Why do women rub their eyes when they get out of bed in the morning?

Because they don't have balls to scratch.

♦

A precocious nine-year-old walked into a bar and yelled to the waitress to bring him a Scotch on the rocks.

"What do you want to do?" asked the waitress. "Get me in trouble?"

"Maybe later," replied the nine-year-old, "but right now I'd like that drink."

♦

There were three couples who approached the local priest because they wanted to join the Catholic church. And he said, "Well, you can join the church, but to be able to join in good standing you have to abstain from sex for thirty days." The three couples agreed to this.

When the thirty days were up, the first couple came in and the priest asked, "How'd you do?" And the husband said, "We did just fine, no problems at all." The priest said, "Well, that's just great. You can come into the church in good standing."

The second couple entered and the priest said, "How'd you do?" The wife said, "Well, we did pretty well. It was really a tough fight, but we did okay." And the priest said, "Well, that's just great. You can come into the church in good standing."

The third couple came in, and when the priest asked how they had done, the husband said, "Well, Father, we did just fine until the twenty-seventh day—my wife bent over to pick up a head of lettuce. I couldn't stand it any longer, and I just put it to her right there." And the priest said, "Well, I'm sorry, you can't come into the church in good standing." And the young man said, "I know. We can't go back into the A & P again, either."

♦

Do you know what the potato chip said to the battery?

If you're Eveready, I'm Frito Lay!

♦

Why can't gypsies have babies?

Because their husbands have crystal balls.

♦

Why can't witches have babies?

Because their husbands have holloweenies.

♦

An eighty-five-year-old man went to the doctor for a physical. After examining the man, the doctor said, "I can hardly believe this! You have the body of a forty-year-old man. You could live quite a long time. How old was your father when he died?"

"Dad's still alive," replied the patient. "He's a hundred and five and still works five days a week."

"Incredible," said the doctor. "How old was your grandfather when he died?"

"Granddaddy's still alive, too. He's a hundred twenty-nine years old and set to marry a twenty-two-year-old girl this Saturday."

"Why ever would a hundred-twenty-nine-year-old man want to get married?"

"Who said he *wants* to get married?"

♦

There is this man and he walks into a patent office and he has a cookie with him. He says that he wants to patent this cookie. And the guy in the patent office says, "Well, what do you mean, patent a cookie? Cookies have been out for years and there are lots and lots of cookies patented. We certainly don't need any more." The man says, "Well, listen. This cookie is something special, something very, very special." And the other man goes, "Well, what's so special about this cookie?" And the first man says, "This cookie tastes just like pussy." And the other says, "Oh, I don't believe it." And the guy that brought the cookie in says, "Taste it, taste it for yourself." So the second man takes a great big bite out of the cookie and he spits it out and he says, "This cookie tastes like shit." And the first man says, "Turn it around."

♦

Do you know what a Cinderella 10 is?

A girl who can fuck and suck all night and then turn into a six-pack after the ball.

♦

A little boy accompanied his swinging parents to a nudist colony for the first time. After looking around for a few minutes, the boy asked his father why some men had big ones and some men had small ones.

Rather than go into a long explanation, the father replied, "The men that have big ones are smart, and the men that have small ones are stupid."

Buying his father's explanation, the boy went off to explore his new surroundings. Time passed and he finally came across his father again.

"Where's your mom, son?"

"Oh," the boy answered, "she's behind the bushes talking to some stupid guy who's getting smarter by the minute."

♦

How far could you see if you had a twelve-inch prick growing out of your forehead?

You couldn't see at all, because the balls would be in your eyes.

♦

What is the difference between like and love?

Spit or swallow.

Pea-Brained Poles

Why do pigeons fly over Poland upside down?

Because there's nothing worth shitting on.

♦

How do you confuse a Pole?

Put him in a round room and tell him to piss in the corner.

♦

Did you hear about the Polish naturalist who thought a spread eagle was an extinct bird?

♦

We all know that the pope is Polish. But did you know that he has a pair of little purple slippers with T.G.I.F. embroidered on the toes? Do you know what T.G.I.F. stands for?

Toes go in first.

♦

Do you know what happened to the Pole when he picked his nose?

His brains caved in.

♦

A Polish girl goes to the gynecologist. She gets up on the table and spreads her legs. The doctor looks her over and can't believe how badly she has taken care of herself.

"When was the last time you had a checkup?" the doctor asks.

Embarrassed, the Polish girl replies, "I haven't had any Czechs, but I've had a few Hungarians."

♦

A Pole driving a convertible sports car is stopped for a red light. A cop on a motorcycle stops beside him. The cop looks over and notices the Pole's backseat is full of penguins with cameras around their little necks. He turns to the Pole and says, "All right, wise guy, bring those penguins back to the zoo, and don't let me see ya pull a stunt like this again. Or next time I'll run ya in. Now get goin'." Frightened, the Pole drives off in the direction of the zoo.

The very next day, the same cop comes across the same car, with the same guy at the wheel. Sure enough, there are the penguins in the backseat, only this time they're wearing baseball caps on their tiny heads.

"Okay, buddy, what's the big idea? I told you if you didn't take those penguins back to the zoo I'd run you in!"

"But, Officer, I did bring them to the zoo."

"Well?" asks the cop.

"So today I'm bringing them to the ball game!"

♦

If Jesus were Polish, what would be his first miracle?

He'd make a blind man deaf.

♦

A Pole went hunting one day and came across a beautiful young woman who was sunbathing nude on a rock. He took one look at her and said, "Are you game?"

Slyly, she replied, "Sure am, big boy."

So he shot her.

♦

A nun went to her mother superior to complain about the language the construction workers who were working next to the convent were using. Sister Margaret was Polish, so the mother superior was used to breaking things down for her.

"Sister Margaret, don't get so upset. Those

men are just people of the earth. They call a spade a spade," the mother superior explained patiently.

Still agitated, Sister Margaret replied, "Oh no, they don't, Mother—they call it a fuckin' shovel!"

♦

Why do they cut pizza into four slices in Poland?

Because they feel the average Pole can't eat eight.

♦

Two fighter pilots, one Polish-American, one German, get into a dogfight over Allied territory. Somehow the Pole downs the German, but he feels so bad about putting the German in the hospital that he has to go visit him. He finds the German in the intensive-care ward, his right leg amputated.

"Gee, I feel so bad, Hans. Is there anything I can do for you?" the Pole asks.

"Well, there is one thing you might do," the German replies. "The leg they removed from me is down in the morgue. If you could take it with you, and the next time you fly over Germany drop it out for me . . ."

"Sure," says the Pole, confused at the request. "No problem."

So the Pole drops the leg over Germany on

his next flight out. He still feels bad about the German, however, so he goes back to visit him again. When he arrives he finds that the German's other leg has been removed. Pity overwhelms him again.

"Hans, look what they've done to you! Is there anything I can do for you now that I'm here?"

"Well, I'd really appreciate it if you could drop my left leg where you dropped its mate."

Still not understanding the German's reasoning, he agrees and performs the request.

Feelings of guilt still linger with the Pole. So he returns to visit the crippled German. The Pole, being very emotional, breaks down at the sight of the poor German. This time his right arm is gone. But before the Pole can say a word, the German begs him to take his arm and do what he did with the rest of his severed limbs.

The Pole's face suddenly becomes clouded and he says accusingly, "All this time I was trying to figure it out, but now I think I've got it. What's the big idea? You trying to escape or something?"

♦

Why didn't the Polish woman wear tight jeans on her trip through Australia?

Because she was afraid of causing a bushfire.

♦

Did you hear about the Polish jazz musician?

He was only in it for the money.

♦

A Pole goes to an eye doctor to be fitted for glasses. The doctor sits him in a chair in front of an eye chart and tells the Pole to cover one of his eyes with one hand. But instead of doing as the doctor showed him, the Pole makes a saluting motion over his right eye.

The doctor tries to show the man twice more what is expected of him and finally gives up. Losing all patience, the doctor fashions a mask out of a brown paper bag, with one eye cut out. Fitting it over the Pole's head, the doctor asks, "How's that feel, Mr. Wororski?"

The Pole hesitates for a moment and says, "It feels fine, Doc, but I was really hoping for something a little more fashionable, maybe something in a wire frame."

Fruits and Nuts

Did you know that thirty percent of the gays in America were born that way? The other seventy percent were sucked into it.

♦

Do you know what the miracle of AIDS is?

It turns fruits into vegetables.

♦

Do you know what you call a gay bar without any bar stools?

A fruit stand.

♦

How does Anita Bryant spell relief?

A-I-D-S.

♦

What do you call a hamburger joint frequented by gays?

Burger Queen.

♦

What do lesbians need to open up a gay bar?

A licker license.

♦

Have you heard what GAY really stands for?

Got Aids Yet?

♦

Did you hear about the newest consumer scare in San Francisco?

A scorned gay slipped Perma Bond into all the K-Y Jelly tubes.

♦

Four gay men are sitting in a Jacuzzi when suddenly they notice a glob of sperm float to the surface. The oldest of the group turns and shrieks, "All right, which one of you bitches farted?"

♦

How do you quiet a gay baby?

Shove a pacifier up its ass.

♦

A man went to the doctor one day complaining that he thought he was gay.

"What makes you think you're gay?" asked the doctor.

"Well," said the man, "my grandfather was gay."

The doctor explained that he didn't think sexual preference was hereditary.

"I see," replied the man, "but my father was also gay."

The doctor said that he thought this was quite unusual, but it didn't necessarily mean that the man was gay.

"Okay," said the man, "but my brother is gay, too."

"My goodness!" exclaimed the doctor. "Doesn't anyone in your family have sex with women?"

"Oh yes," replied the man. "My sister."

◆

Do you know what you call two gays on skateboards?

Roll Aids.

◆

A gay man was standing in front of his bathroom mirror brushing his teeth when his gums started to bleed. "Thank God," he said to himself. "Safe for another month."

♦

An English officer is assigned to a detachment of American soldiers in a foreign country. The American officer in charge comes over to greet the newcomer.

"Officer Hayes," the American says, "you're going to like it here in our camp. I mean, we don't just sit around and watch the grass grow while waiting for orders. Take Monday nights. On Monday night we all get rip-roaring drunk."

"Well, that leaves me out," the Englishman says stiffly. "I don't drink."

"Well," continues the American, "on Tuesday night we all get wrecked on weed."

"Sorry," says the Englishman. "I don't do that, either."

"Not to worry, 'cause on Wednesday we really have a ball, and bring in the chicks from the nearby village. That's when all the real fun begins."

"Well, I hate to disappoint you, old chap, but I don't go around with cheap women," the Englishman says flatly.

"Don't go around with cheap women? You're not one of those queers, are you?"

Highly insulted, the Englishman says, "Of course not!"

The American whistles through his teeth and says, "Well, for sure you're not gonna like Thursday night!"

♦

Did you hear about the gay man who got the mumps?

He told his lover they were expecting.

♦

Have you heard about the gay sperm whale in the Florida Keys?

He bit the head off a submarine and ate the seamen.

♦

What do you call a gay midget?

Sweet and low.

♦

What did one lesbian say to the other at the gay bar?

"Care to come back to my place for some twat-tails?"

♦

Have you heard about the new convenience food product that all the gays are buying?

It's called Semen Helper.

Racial Mixtures

Why are there so many virgins in Ireland?

Because all the pricks are over here.

♦

What's more confusing than a Chinese fire drill?

Father's Day in Harlem.

♦

What do you call a Mexican woman with no legs?

Cuntsuelo.

♦

What do heads of lettuce and noses have in common?

Mexicans pick them both.

♦

What do you call a guy who's half Indian and half Chinese?

Uglee.

♦

What's long, white, and useless on a woman?

An Irishman.

♦

What do you call a Mexican without any arms or legs?

Trustworthy.

♦

Do you know why the Indians were here first?

Because they had reservations.

♦

What happens to an Indian who drinks too much tea?

He drowns in his teepee.

♦

A man in South Dakota walks into a bar and asks for a drink. The bartender says, "Sorry, we don't serve Indians here."

"But I'm not an Indian," the man replies.

"Prove it."

"How?"

♦

A Jew, a Protestant, and a Catholic died and were waiting at the Pearly Gates. Saint Peter came out to interview them.

"You!" he said to the Jew. "You liked money so much you called your wife Penny. To hell with you!"

The Protestant stepped up. "And you!" Saint Peter bellowed. "You liked liquor so much you called your wife Sherry. To hell with you!"

"Wait a minute," he called to the Catholic. "Why are you following them?"

"I don't stand a chance," the Catholic explained. "My wife's name is Fanny."

♦

What do you get when you cross a black hooker with a Chinaman?

A woman who will suck your shirts.

♦

Why do WASPs throw their garbage away in clear plastic bags?

So that Puerto Ricans can go window-shopping.

♦

Do you know why they have such a low suicide rate in Puerto Rico?

Because you can't kill yourself jumping out of a basement window.

♦

What are the first four words a Puerto Rican child learns?

"Give me your wallet!"

♦

Do you know what makes a man a gentleman in Greece?

He's a man who takes a girl out at least five times before he propositions her younger brother.